The Illustrated Guide to Dyslexia and Its Amazing People

_ _

First published in 2018
by Jessica Kingsley Publishers
73 Collier Street
London N1 9BE, UK
and
400 Market Street, Suite 400
Philadelphia, PA 19106, USA

www.jkp.com

Library of Congress Cataloging in Publication Data
A CIP catalog record for this book is available from the Library of Congress

British Library Cataloguing in Publication Data
A CIP catalogue record for this book is available from the British Library

ISBN 978 1 78592 330 2
eISBN 978 1 78450 647 6

Printed and bound in China

The Illustrated Guide to Dyslexia
and Its Amazing People

Kate Power & Kathy Iwanczak Forsyth
Foreword by Richard Rogers

London and Philadelphia

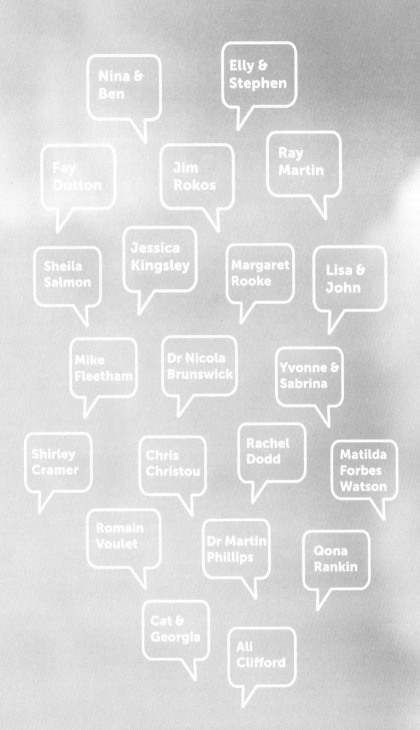

What a great example of dyslexic thinking!

The Lloyd's Building, London, by Richard Rogers, Architect. Service features, including pipes and lifts, were designed to be on the exterior, giving rise to the nickname 'The Inside-Out building'.

Foreword

When I was a schoolboy in the 1940s, dyslexia was not known about or understood, so like many others I was labelled as stupid. Thankfully, dyslexia is now recognised as a specific learning disability, and with the right teaching most dyslexics learn to read and write. However, even now, dyslexia is not fully understood by the experts; there is still a lot of work to be done.

As a 10-year-old boy who could not read, write or spell very well, for a while I lost all self-confidence. I was very unhappy. However, things got better with support from loving parents and a particular teacher who told me to 'just write and stop worrying about if someone can read it'. I was a hard worker, and learnt quickly not to believe people who told me that I could not do something. I just had to find another way to do it.

The Illustrated Guide to Dyslexia and Its Amazing People is a beautiful book created by Kate and Kathy. It was designed to explain to their dyslexic children what dyslexia means. It also aims to inspire and to motivate them when things get hard and frustrating. Sometimes dyslexia does not make life easy. It is based on their own experience of working with their children, and from books, online research, documentaries and radio interviews. It is a basic introduction to help you understand what dyslexia is and how it can affect you, and concludes with a good dollop of how wonderful the end result can be.

Dyslexics have a great way of looking at a problem and turning it on its head. Don't give up.

Richard Rogers, Architect

Why we wrote this book

You + Me

Conventional dyslexia books have too many words!

This illustrated guide to dyslexia is designed
to be enjoyed with your youngster. It will explain to both of
you the individual issues and strengths dyslexia presents,
provide some useful tips and break down barriers.

So curl up on the sofa with this book, a cuppa and an amazing
dyslexic and let the conversation unfold...

This book is for

YOU

Nice to
meet you.

There are so
many
of us

You are not alone.

bout 1 in 10 of us are amazing (dyslexic).

> It means
> a difficulty
> with words.

Dyslexia

comes from the Greek language:
'Dys' meaning difficulty, 'lexia' meaning words.

It's not just about finding reading, writing and spelling tricky.
It can also affect speaking, remembering, understanding, speed,
movement and basic maths. It can range from mild to severe.

The great news is that with good teaching most dyslexics learn to read.

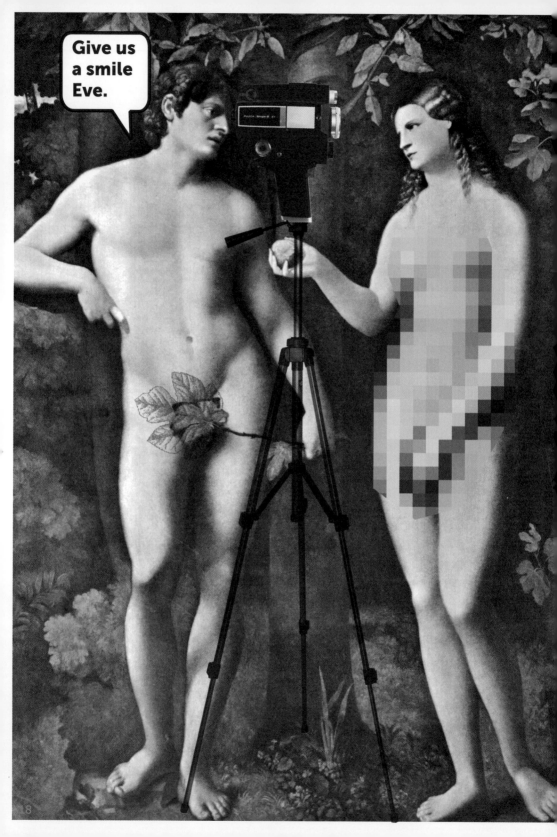

The BIG message

Dyslexia is different for everybody

Use this guide to weed out what dyslexia means for you and discover the tools you need to

blossom

Dyslexia runs in families

Dyslexia is inherited, like all your characteristics

Who's **amazing** in your family?

Mum?

You

Dad?

Brother?

Sister?

Cousin?

Granny?

Auntie?

Let's get inside your head!

Using brain scans, scientists can see that dyslexics think in a different way. This can have some rather lovely side effects.

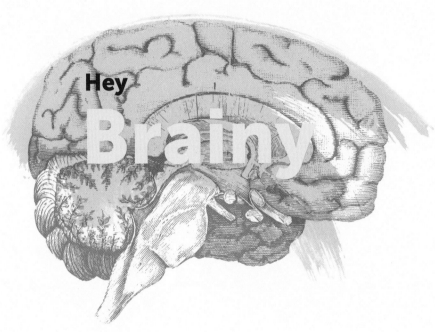

Hey **Brainy**

Creative
Imaginative
Story telling
Inventive
Connecting ideas
Visionary
Seeing the bigger picture
Problem solving
Free thinking
Thoughtful
Thinking in 3D
Passionate

Don't be pigeon-holed by dyslexia.

23

Non-dyslexic straight thinking

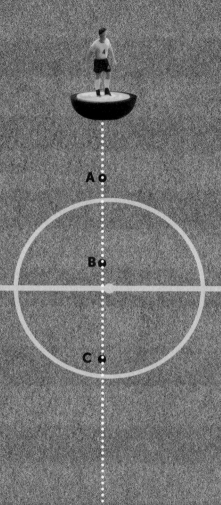

A •

B •

C •

Goal !

Be a game changer!

Dyslexic thinking is like a pinball machine, information bounces around your brain and can lead to some winning ideas.

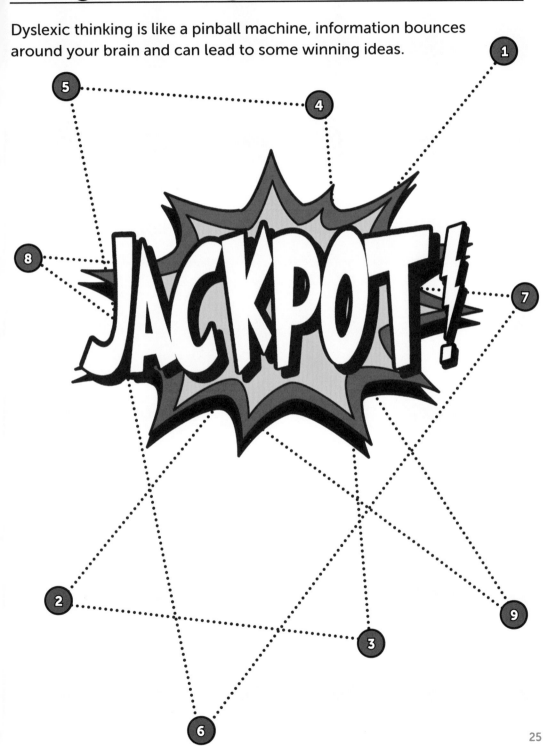

Some early clues to dyslexia

But not a definitive checklist that you are dyslexic.

Nippers
- Not crawling as a baby
- Late to start talking
- Putting shoes on the wrong feet
- Falling over and bumping into things

Whipper-snappers
- Wrongly accused of not listening or paying attention
- Surprising people by the really clever and imaginative things you say

Lacking self-confidence

Using your fingers to do easy maths

Taking longer than anyone else to do your written work

Forgetting instructions

Making mistakes when you read

Struggling to organise your social life

Teeny-boppers

Another BIG wonderful message

Dyslexia is a different way of learning and thinking

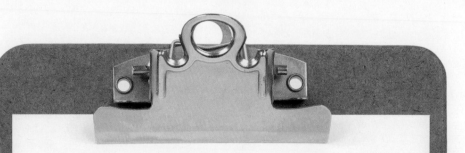

If you think your child might be dyslexic

Talk to their teacher and the school's learning support team.

Check their eyesight at the optician.

Get advice from their family doctor.

Find a professional who can assess for dyslexia.

Check online for your national dyslexia organisation to get guidance and support.

While assessing for dyslexia, check for other learning difficulties, like Asperger syndrome (AS), attention deficit hyperactivity disorder (ADHD), dyspraxia and dyscalculia, as you can have dyslexia alone or alongside one of these.

Dr. Dashing advises

Assessment without delay, professional advice, a supportive elder, a positive attitude and lots of hard work.

Have your say

This part of the book is to help you understand what dyslexia means for you, and to help you explain to others how dyslexia affects you and your learning.

On the following pages, you will find empty speech bubbles. Tick or cross if you can relate to what's been said and perhaps talk about how it makes you feel.

You will also find, at the bottom of each page, red boxes containing top tips and black boxes with useful website addresses.

Pencil at the ready!

 Top Tips   Websites we found useful

What gets you in a pickle?

Poppy needs to see a word many times before she remembers it

Most non-dyslexics only need to see a word about 6 times before they recognise it, but some dyslexics need to see a word again and...

again again again again again again again again again again again again again again
again again again again again again again again again again again again again again
again again again again again again again again again again again again again again
again again again again again again again again again again again again again again
again again again again again again again again again again again again again again
again again again again again again again again again again again again again again
again again again again again again again again again again again again again again
again again again again again again again again again again again again again again
again again again again again again again again again again again again again again
again again again again again again again again again again again again again again
again again again again again again again again again again again again again again
again again again again again again again again again again again again again again

Find a learning method that works for you, and practise daily. 'Perfect' practice makes perfect.

Noah does not always know what letter shapes sound like

To read you need to know the sound of the letter you are looking at. This is called letter and sound association. Sound familiar?

I recognise the letter but I can't remember what it sounds like.

It's the duh sound.

You can make your own phonics card game and then play with a friend.

'Miss...what shall I do next?'

Even though Reggie understands the set of instructions, as soon as he starts the first task he can't remember what to do next.

Get your reading book out,

turn to page 7,

read paragraph 2 and

colour in the picture.

OK done... forgot page number...

ummm, what next...

what did she say?

Patience is a virtue.
Keep lists short and sweet.

When Ned reads, **every third** word **disappears. When** Ned **reads, every** third **word disappears.** When **Ned reads,** every **third word** disappears.

For others, words can flash, jiggle or run off the page... Arghhh!

Use coloured paper and overlays or tinted glasses.

www.irlen.com

Blen-ding

Molly finds it really tough to know when and where to blend sounds.

Find a tutor or use specially designed learning recipes.

www.patoss-dyslexia.org
www.toe-by-toe.co.uk
www.wordshark.co.uk

~~Erorr~~ ~~Errer~~ Error detection

When checking his work, Bones has problems spotting his mistakes.

Go fetch your ideas!
Focus on them, and let
spellcheck do the rest.

Ziggy gets spaced out following a storyline

If only we spelt all words how they sounded!

Duz meening thuh get becoz
thuh ov storee lost

Your reading partner can help by giving you the bigger picture and pointing out tricky words.

Read comics, magazines and graphic novels – stuff that interests you.

yur

sew   bizzy

wurking   eech

owt   wurd ?

Jonny likes to read books that have more space between the lines and bigger letters

Your homework is to find out what works best for you.

12 pt and 14 pt great choice of font size ....
Perfect line spacing 1.5 ....

Dear Mrs Freeman, I love you so,
I am so sorry to see you go
skidding across the room on my banana skin
I should have put it in the compost bin!

By Reggie Power, age 9

A*
Excellent work

Choose preferred size and line spacing on e-readers.

Georgie finds it easier to read fonts without flicky bits (serifs), like Arial, rather than with serifs, like Times

A font is a particular design of type. Some are easier to read than others. This book uses Museo Sans. What's your favourite?

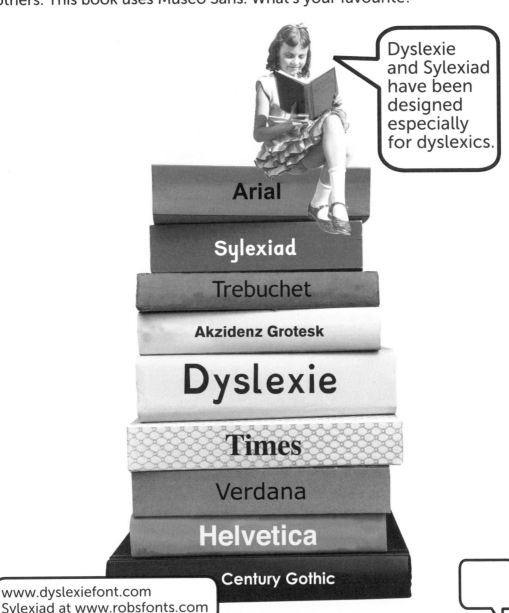

Dyslexie and Sylexiad have been designed especially for dyslexics.

Arial

Sylexiad

Trebuchet

Akzidenz Grotesk

Dyslexie

Times

Verdana

Helvetica

Century Gothic

www.dyslexiefont.com
Sylexiad at www.robsfonts.com

bed

44

Leo draws and writes his letters and words the wrong way round

Leonardo Da Vinci, the artist, architect, engineer and scientist, wrote most of his personal notes in mirror writing.

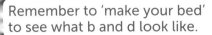
Remember to 'make your bed' to see what b and d look like.

Wot **?**

were they thinking when they decided
not to spell some words as they sound?

www.wordshark.co.uk

Fred battles with spelling

He spells words as they sound, leaves out letters, adds letters, puts letters in the wrong order and sometimes his spelling is utter nonsense!

Find words within words.
Learn spellings using all your senses.
Say it out loud, write it down big and small, strut around writing it in the air!

Tom's handwriting is messy

Some days his writing is unreadable and his letters are inconsistent. He mixes up his upper and lower cases and his letter shapes and sizes are irregular. It makes it very difficult to get ideas and thoughts onto paper.

And my hand gets tired and hurts when I write.

Learn to type! In exams make sure you get extra time, or a scribe, for written work. Check posture, angle of paper, pencil grip, HB pencil, ruled paper.

Touch-type Read and Spell
www.readandspell.com

Fin finds learning foreign languages mind boggling!

Grammar can be hard enough in your own mother tongue. However, persevere as it's good to broaden your horizons and extremely handy on holiday!

Ooo la la!

Français

You may find Spanish, Italian and German easier to learn as they are more phonetic languages.

Junie amusingly says one thing but means another!

I've got the fire distinguisher, bellowed Mrs. Junie Malaprop.

I think she means fire extinguisher darling!

Deep breath and refocus!

Reggie 'unbeknowingly' invents his own words for things!

Nice knee cheeks!

Also known as calves

Enjoy the poetry within you!

Pierre was lost for words

Although he can see exactly where the wooden spoon is, in his mind he can't find the word 'table' to answer the question.

It's on the... thingy-me-bob. You know the wotsit.

Don't stress!

52

Jim's missed the boat — again!

He has trouble planning and organising his social scene. He didn't mean to miss his date, but some girls just don't wait around!

Get a planner, set alarms on your phone, write notes to yourself.

Raun is always running late

He finds it hard to grasp the concept of time, and always underestimates how long things take.

Go digital if you struggle with analogue.
Give yourself extra time.

Peter is pants at getting things in the right order

He finds it hard to remember the alphabet, days of the week, months of the year and times tables.

Use silly songs and funny games to help remember.

Lulu dances to her own beat

Some cool cats are uncoordinated and can't remember a sequence.
The upside is that you may find your own original and better way.

Better to freestyle baby!

Ralph's grammar does not stick

Complete your homework while it's fresh in your mind. Ask your teacher or find tutorials online if you don't understand the rules.

Butterfingers

If there is something for Ted to drop, bump into or fall over, he will!

Barney's sums don't add up

He battles with basic arithmetic, times tables and maths formula.
He gets in a muddle with counting, estimating and measuring, and
can't see the relationship between numbers.

Learn and use the times table grid.
Practise your maths at the shops with
your money. Make sure you use the
same methods at home and school.

www.numbershark.co.uk

Sam's nightmare is a blank page

He finds it hard to get his thoughts onto paper.

Get started with spider diagrams and
mindmaps and use assisted technology.

Mishearing, muddling and misinterpretation

Some dyslexics with perfect hearing muddle what they hear, in the same way that some dyslexics with perfect eyesight muddle what they read. Fran can hear what is said but her mind interprets another meaning. She also finds it hard to follow a conversation when there is background noise.

Where did you get that hat?

Some folks work better in silence and prefer to sit at the front of the class.

Rosie is a daydreamer

So was the brilliant Sir Isaac Newton, who had his best idea, the law of gravity, whilst daydreaming underneath an apple tree.

Your best ideas often come when you are relaxed and free thinking.

Nell has good days and bad days

For no particular reason some days your dyslexia can be more challenging than others.

For best results keep things upbeat, encouraging and stress-free.

The Amazing People and the Jobs They Do

The world is your oyster!

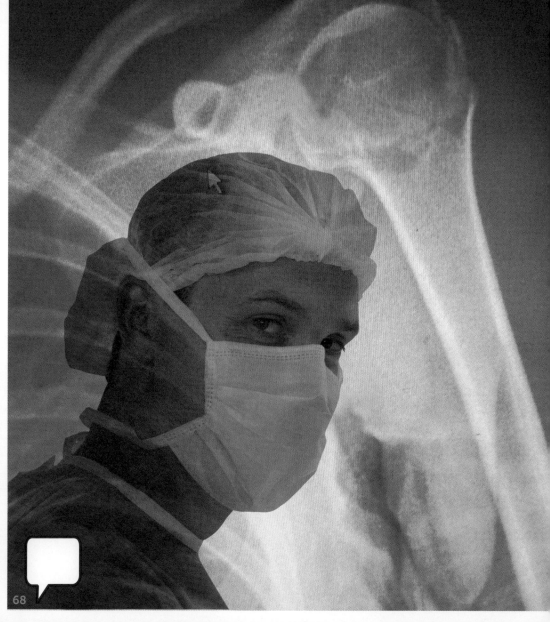

Do you like to fix things?

Consultant orthopaedic surgeon Toby Baring uses his own logic to dissect a problem and then he understands how to fix it. The key player in developing a new X-ray technique 'RSA' to monitor rotator cuff tears. This is the man who puts dislocated shoulders back where they belong!

Do you recall colours as they are?

Dyslexia helps Ab Rogers as a designer – it allows him to see things in three dimensions and remember colours, conversations, tastes and smells with real accuracy.

Can you walk through a building in your mind that hasn't been built yet?

Richard Rogers learnt early on that when people said something was impossible, he shouldn't believe them. This made him a trier and he's still trying.

Le Centre Pompidou – magnifique!

Do you think different?

Dyslexia is commonplace in the creative industries, embracing people who think differently. Dyslexics can see what ordinary people can't. Who would want to be ordinary? Not Chris Arnold.

Can you talk the talk?

Sean Douglas, 'Chief Operating Dyslexic' and founder of The Codpast, hosts facinating podcasts for students and adults with dyslexia. Check out the fresh and inspiring website and podcast for up-to-the-minute dyslexic news and views.

ON AIR

17   4:08

7

Do you have ideas by the metre?

Like Henry Franks, who transforms everyday objects into something wonderfully extraordinary. His 'Ideas by the Metre' table lets you sketch until you've nailed that design!

Is your imagination popping with magical fantastical artistry?

You can peek inside Kristjana S Williams' imagination through her art and her book **The Wonder Garden**. It's full of curious habitats and enchanting creatures.

Is the music in you?

It is in Dave Williamson, who plays trombone with Mumford & Sons. Since he was 6 years old music has been everything to him, he feels a connection to it and composing melodies in his head comes easily to him.

You're one cool cat Dave!

Can you turn a shoe dream into high-heeled reality?

Natacha Marro has, and now makes shoes for the stars. Dyslexia made her focus on what she is good at. When Natacha's in her workshop making shoes, she's in her comfort zone. It's a magical place! Do something you love!

Does the field come into focus, the more specialised the subject?

It did for Dr. Brian Darby BEng, MSc, PhD, who achieved in academics and athletics. He currently holds 18 medals from the British National Masters, European Masters and World Masters Championships. Once Brian had found his subject and his style of learning, nobody could keep up with him.

Are you a team player?

Kenny Logan is! When learning to read, the Scottish rugby player, sports entrepreneur and dyslexia campaigner compared his brain to 'a bucket with a hole in it, the words didn't stay in'. However, it's never too late to tackle the problem. Kenny now champions the STEP physical literacy programme, connecting exercise and literacy.

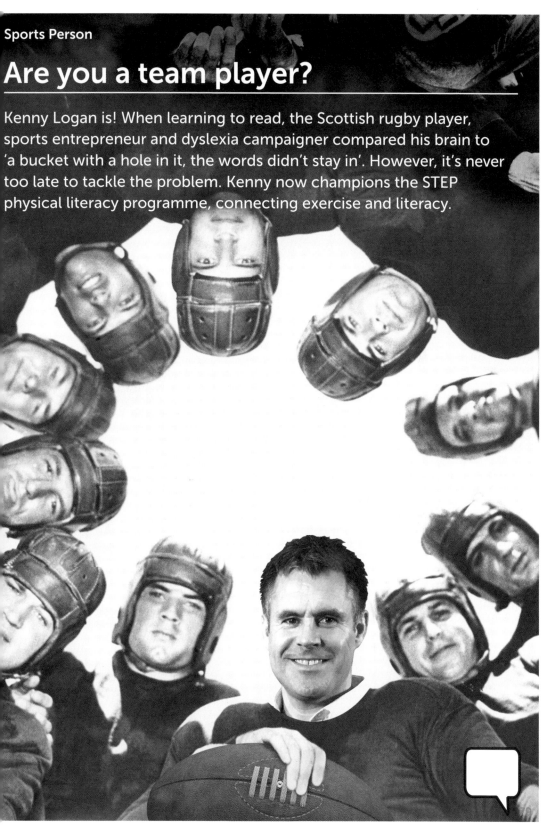

Do you have fast reflexes?

Sir Jackie Stewart, OBE, known as the 'Flying Scot', is one of Formula 1's greatest racing drivers. He's also a TV presenter, businessman, the founder of the Race Against Dementia Foundation and President of Dyslexia Scotland. Having hidden his struggles with reading and writing for 42 years, it was a relief to be finally assessed for dyslexia at the same time as his son. He has always looked for ways to do things a bit differently from his competition, with winning results!

Do you have the need for speed?

'Chief Bolt' Kenny Handkammer does! He was chief mechanic at Red Bull Racing, and part of the team that broke the record for the fastest pitstop at the US Grand Prix in 2013. He now has his sleeves rolled up at Tesla Motors.

Can you see subtle connections?

As head of Global Innovation Design at the Royal College of Art, Dr. Jonathan Edelman, PhD, MFA, is on a mission to find solutions to the world's big problems. He teaches postgraduates to look at an issue, dissect it and then solve it mechanically with an object, intellectually by changing people's perceptions, and poetically by making it beautiful in the eyes of the beholder.

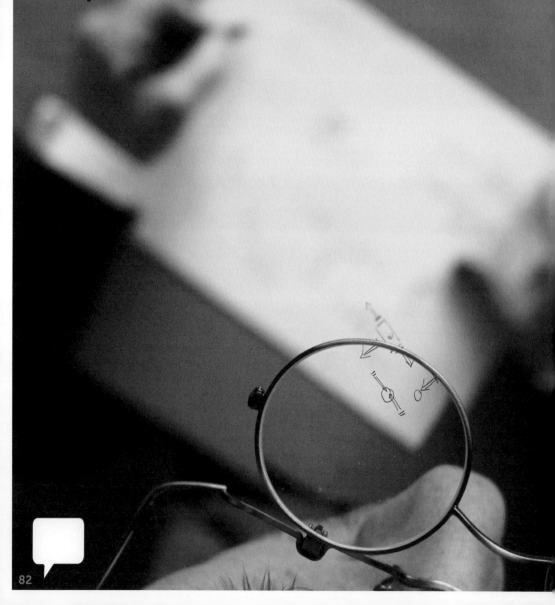

Can you see the potential in others?

Mr. Fletcher's dyslexia has given him the ability to understand his students who find learning difficult, and to encourage them to keep trying and focus on the things they are good at. It makes you a resiliant adult.

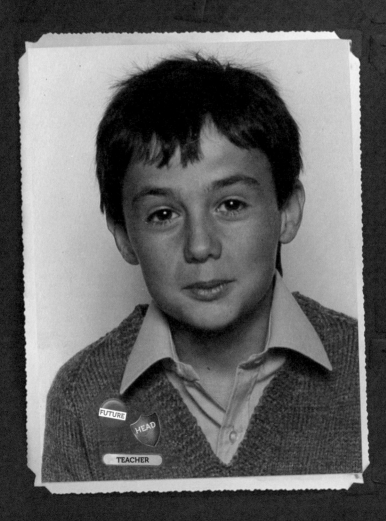

Stunt Co-ordinator

Have you found what lights your fire?

Rob Inch is pictured here as the stunt double for Antonio Banderas in The Legend Of Zorro. As a child, Rob found it hard to learn anything that he was not interested in, but when he was interested he came out all guns blazing!

Are you passionate about a cause?

Jim Rokos set up 'Dyslexic Design' to exhibit and celebrate the connection between dyslexia and creativity. To show young dyslexics who feel like ugly ducklings the beautiful swans they will become. Artfully said.

Actor
Architect
Artist
Artisan
Astronomer
Author
Barrister
Boat Captain
Builder
Business Executive
Carpenter
Chemist
Chef
Coder
Comedian
Computer Networker
Computer Programmer
Dancer
Dentist
Designer
Driver
Electrician
Engineer
Entrepreneur
Fashion Designer
Film Director
Graphic Designer
Inventor
Landscape Gardener
Mechanic
Orthodontist
Photographer
Pilot
Plumber
Physicist
Radiologist
Scientist
Singer
Surgeon
Teacher
Vet
Zoologist

Good jobs for dyslexic strengths

The last BIG message

As a dyslexic you learn that you have to work hard.
This is a good ethos for life.

Try your best

Ask for help

Be true to yourself

& join our club!

Upload your photos and achievements on Instagram
#amazingdyslexic

Find us on Instagram
@amazingdyslexic

Find us on Twitter
@amazingdyslexic

Facebook
amazing dyslexic

How your grown-up can help you beat dyslexia!

1. Being read to from a young age gives you an enjoyment of stories, and a great vocabulary.

2. While you read, chat about the story to make you want to read on.

3. Have tricky words pointed out before to keep the story moving.

4. Nudge your grown-up to recognise and praise your effort!

5. Try to relate the story to things that have happened to you.

6. If you feel you are struggling more than your friends, talk to someone, as getting help earlier is better.

7. Make sure you understand what you're learning. It's hard to remember what you don't get.

8. Read out loud for 15 minutes a day, at least 4 times a week. This will make a huge difference.

9. Once you can read, keep practising reading out loud, to help you gain speed.

10. And keep the bedtime stories going as long as possible. It's wonderful being read to and it increases your vocabulary.

Create wacky rhymes to remember difficult times tables.

I ate and I ate and was sick on the floor

8x8 is 64

Give a tricky word an image to make sense of the spelling.

To spell **'necessary'** think one coffee and two sugars. (one c and two s's)

Think about James covered in jam and never forget his name!

Mnemonic memory joggers.

Could Would Should

Oh Lucky Duck

Overcoming Dyslexia by Sally Shaywitz, MD.
This is a fabulous book! It will help you understand how the brain works when we read, how to teach reading and how dyslexics need to be taught.

What Is Dyslexia? by Alan M. Hultquist.
Simply and clearly explains dyslexia.

Creative, Successful, Dyslexic by Margaret Rooke.
A wonderful and inspiring book that gives an insight into the lives of 23 famous dyslexics.

Dyslexia: A parents' guide to dyslexia, dyspraxia and other learning difficulties by Dr. V. Muter and Dr. H. Likierman.
A great book to give you an overview of dyslexia, dyspraxia and other learning difficulties. It gives good advice.

Alpha to Omega: The A–Z of Teaching Reading, Writing and Spelling by Dyslexia Action. Auntie Sheila swore by this book to help teach children to read.

Handwriting...are you concerned? by Beverly Scheib. Some useful tips.

The Dyslexic Advantage by Dr. Brock L. Eide and Dr. Frenetter F. Eide. This book will get you really excited about the advantages to being dyslexic!

Overcoming Dyslexia by Dr. Beve Hornsby. A great book by a pioneer in the field.

The Vicar of Nibbleswick by Roald Dahl. A fun story about dyslexia by the amazing Roald Dahl.

Professional organisations for further help

UK and Ireland

The British Dyslexia Association
www.bdadyslexia.org.uk

Dyslexia Scotland
www.dyslexiascotland.org.uk

Dyslecsia Cymru
www.walesdyslexia.org.uk

Northern Ireland Dyslexia Association
www.nida.org.uk

Helen Arkell Dyslexia Centre
www.arkellcentre.org.uk

Dyslexia Association of Ireland
www.dyslexia.ie

Europe

European Dyslexia Association
www.eda-info.eu

USA and Canada

International Dyslexia Association
www.interdys.org

Canada Dyslexia Association
www.dyslexiaassociation.ca

Australia

Australian Dyslexia Association
www.dyslexiaassociation.org.au

New Zealand

Dyslexia Foundation of New Zealand
www.dyslexiafoundation.org.nz

Who are Kate and Kathy?

Kate is a creative, a curator of beautiful things, who is surrounded by amazing dyslexics! After graduating from Camberwell College of Art, she then went on to set up Applied Arts Agency to promote great design. Kate now works at a contemporary art gallery.

Kathy works at Youmeus, London. As an industrial stylist she provides colour, material and lifestyle mapping to inform product and brand experience opportunities. She has two dyslexic children.

PHOTO CREDITS

of related interest

CREATIVE, SUCCESSFUL, DYSLEXIC
23 High Achievers Share Their Stories
Margaret Rooke
Foreword by Mollie King
ISBN 978 1 78592 060 8
eISBN 978 1 78450 163 1

DYSLEXIA IS MY SUPERPOWER
(Most of the Time)
Margaret Rooke
ISBN 978 1 78592 299 2
eISBN 978 1 78450 606 3

I DON'T LIKE READING!
Lisabeth Emlyn Clark
ISBN 978 1 78592 354 8
eISBN 978 1 78450 693 3

CAN I TELL YOU ABOUT DYSLEXIA?
A guide for friends, family and professionals
Alan M. Hultquist
Illustrated by Bill Tulp
ISBN 978 1 84905 952 7
eISBN 978 0 85700 810 7